X

–Fast Tracks

–Formula 1 Racing

A. T. McKenna

visit us at
www.abdopub.com

Published by Abdo & Daughters, 4940 Viking Drive, Suite 622, Edina, Minnesota 55435.
Copyright © 1998 by Abdo Consulting Group, Inc., Pentagon Tower, P.O. Box 36036, Minneapolis, Minnesota 55435 USA. International copyrights reserved in all countries. No part of this book may be reproduced in any form without written permission from the publisher.

Printed in the United States.

Cover and Interior Photo credits: Allsport USA, Duomo, SportsChrome

Edited by Paul Joseph

Library of Congress Cataloging-in-Publication Data

McKenna, A. T.
   Formula 1 racing / A. T. McKenna.
      p. cm. -- (Fast tracks)
  Includes index.
  Summary: Describes the design and construction of Formula 1 race cars and the action during the international Grand Prix races.
  ISBN 1-56239-838-5
  1. Grand Prix racing--Juvenile literature. 2. Formula One automobiles--Juvenile literature
[1. Automobile racing. 2.Grand Prix racing 3. Formula One automobiles.] I. Title II. Title:
Formula One racing. III Series: McKenna, A. T. Fast tracks.
GV1029.M45 1998
796.72--dc21
                                                         97-29380
                                                          CIP
                                                          AC

-Contents

–Formula 1 Racing

Formula 1 racing is one of the most prestigious forms of auto racing in the world today. This sport, also known as Grand Prix racing, draws racers from all over the world. Grand Prix is French for "Great Prize."

In the beginning, Formula 1 racing took place from city to city. Cars started out one by one, and the winner was decided by the amount of time it took the driver to get to the next city. The very first race was from Paris to Rouen in 1895. The race was won by Emile Levassor.

Grand Prix is another name for Formula 1.

The governing body, called the Federation Internationale de l'Automobile (FIA), decided to create a series of races called the World Championship. A governing body, such as FIA, decides the rules and point system for the racing series.

The first official Formula 1 race was held on May 15, 1950, although several countries had their own Grand Prix races for many years before. The race was the British Grand Prix in Silverstone, England.

This first race had drivers from just seven different countries. The countries participating included Italy, France, Argentina, United States, Thailand, Great Britain, and Monaco. Each of these countries held a race in the World Championship, making a total of seven races that year. The winner of the 1950 World Championship was an Italian named Giuseppe Farina. Farina drove an Alfa Romeo car.

Olivier Panis in the 1997 Monaco Grand Prix.

—Formula 1 Circuits

A circuit is another name for race track. Unlike other forms of race car driving, Formula 1 racing takes place mostly on city streets in various countries. About 58 different circuits from 22 different countries have been used for World Championship Grand Prix races. Different countries who have held Formula 1 races include: United States, France, Spain, Argentina, Belgium, Canada, Germany, Great Britain, Italy, Portugal, Austria, Brazil, Japan, South Africa, Australia, the Netherlands, Hungary, Mexico, Monaco, Morocco, Sweden, and Switzerland.

The Monaco Grand Prix, through the streets of Monte Carlo, is one of the best known Formula 1 races. It is the slowest of all the World Championship races. The circuit runs through hotels, shops, restaurants, and apartments of Monte Carlo. This makes the race a challenging one.

Another famous Formula 1 race used to be the Indianapolis 500. The Indianapolis 500 was part of the World Championship from 1950 to 1960. Not many European drivers drove in the Indianapolis 500. They chose to drive the circuits in Europe instead. American Formula 1 drivers won every Indianapolis 500 and claimed all World Championship points for that race.

—On the Road

Many Formula 1 race tracks are located in Europe. The cars are taken to the races by a fancy truck, which is called a transporter. Transporter drivers will drive for many hours and through several countries to get the race car to the track. These drivers are called "truckies." Truckies take very good care of the race cars.

The cars always arrive in excellent condition, with no damage from traveling. There are usually several truckies on each race team. These people look after the transporter tires, refueling, changing oil, and other maintenance.

Since Formula 1 racing takes place all over the world, sometimes the cars must be taken apart and transported to the various race tracks. It can take an average of six hours to strip the cars down. Most cars are then put into huge containers and taken as freight by plane to their destination.

Cars must be able to be taken apart and shipped to other places.

–The Car

Formula 1 cars are small and light in weight, but they are very fast cars. The first component on a Formula 1 car is the body or chassis. The chassis of the car is very strong, but very light. It weighs much less than the person driving it.

The chassis is made from a mold. The mold is lined with several pieces of a material called carbon fiber. The pieces of carbon fiber are woven together to form a frame for the car.

The mold and chassis are then placed in a huge oven called an autoclave. The chassis is cooked at 380 degrees Fahrenheit for one to two hours until it is stiff and strong. The chassis must be very strong to protect the driver if there is a crash. It is the driver's survival cell.

Next, body panels are added. When the body is complete, you can't see any gaps or spaces in between the body pieces. The car looks like it is all one piece.

There are two very fragile pieces, the nose cone and the rear wing. These pieces are usually the last to be attached to the car. Although the rear wing may seem a little flimsy, this carbon fiber piece can withstand downforce pressures of approximately 2,000 pounds (907 kg). Downforce is the amount of air pressure pushing down on the wing. When traveling long distance, the

delicate nose cone and the rear wing are transported separately to avoid damage.

After each race, the car is brought back to the body shop and taken apart. Before the next race, the cars are repainted and put back together. This takes about 36 hours before the car is ready to go again.

Once the body of the car is assembled, the car is given a paint job. The body panels are spray painted in the team colors. Logos of the sponsors are then added. Sponsors are the companies who help to pay for the car.

Logos can have the name of the company and company artwork. Some of the names seen on Formula 1 cars include companies such as Goodyear, Renault, Benetton, Agip, Shell, Brembo, Honda, and Dirt Devil.

Rules specify where the car number should be displayed on the car and the minimum size the number must be. The car number is painted on both sides of the rear wing and on the nose cone of the car so it can be seen from all angles, even the official's tower above the track.

When these brightly colored cars race by on the track at full speed, all that can be seen is a whirl of colors.

Formula I cars are so fast that most times all you can see is a blur of colors.

The inside parts are added on a Formula 1 car as the body panels are fitted in place. These include the engine, fuel system, exhaust system, and cooling system.

The engine on a Formula 1 car is fitted behind the driver's seat. This spot is the center of the car. The engine is limited to a maximum capacity of three liters. These engines help the cars race around the track at speeds of 210 miles per hour (338 kilometers per hour) and higher. The type of engine used in a Formula 1 car is either a V8 or a V10.

Formula 1 cars have fuel tanks which are called fuel cells. The fuel cell is like a bladder. This bladder deforms or changes its shape and becomes flexible if it is hit in an accident. This prevents the fuel cell from rupturing and prevents fuel from splattering out if there is a crash. The fuel cell must be placed on the chassis behind the driver's back. No fuel can be placed in front of the driver.

On a regular car, the exhaust pipes are found in the rear of the car, between the rear wheels. On a Formula 1 car, the exhaust pipes are in the rear of the car also. The exhaust pipes are made of Inconel, an extremely hard steel. Each exhaust system can cost about $5,500.

During the race, the engine gets very hot. The car needs something to help supply cool air to the engine area. This is the

cooling system, made up of an air inlet duct which looks like a snorkel. It is a curving tunnel made of carbon fiber that carries air to the engine. The driver also gets quite hot inside the cockpit. Air vents and fans help keep the driver cool, too.

The interior of a Formula 1 car doesn't look anything like a regular car. The area where the driver sits is called the cockpit. This area has an aluminum steering wheel which is covered with soft felt material so it can be molded to the driver's hand for a precise grip. Steering wheels can cost up to $6,000.

A Formula I cockpit.

On the steering wheel are several multi-colored buttons. What each button does is a closely guarded secret among the race team. However, some of the buttons are standard on all the steering wheels.

A black button is found at the bottom left of the steering wheel. This button is used to turn on the radio to communicate with the team from the track. The yellow button on the lower right is the speed limiter when the driver is in the pit area, along the side of the track.

There are also buttons and levers in other places in the cockpit. There is a red button on the right for the fire extinguisher. There is a red lever in the lower left area of the steering wheel which is to start the car.

Formula 1 cars have three digital screens above the steering wheel. The left screen shows the hydraulic pressure (the pressure of the fluids in the engine). The middle screen shows the car's speed. The screen on the right shows which gear the car is in— 1st, 2nd, 3rd, or 4th.

Formula 1 cars have special seatbelts, called safety harnesses, which make sure the driver won't be moved out of place. A special padded headrest helps prevent injuries to the neck and head in case of an accident.

P. CARPENTIER

Kawnee

Formula I cockpits are very tight to
keep the driver from moving around

LAUREL Spark Plugs

OIL

SPEED LUBE

INTERNAT

EXIT

1976 - First Japanese Grand Prix.

1967 - First Canadian Grand Prix.

1962 - First Mexican Grand Prix.

1 2 3 4

1959 - First United States Grand Prix

1958 - First Moroccan Grand Prix. It was also the only Moroccan Grand Prix.

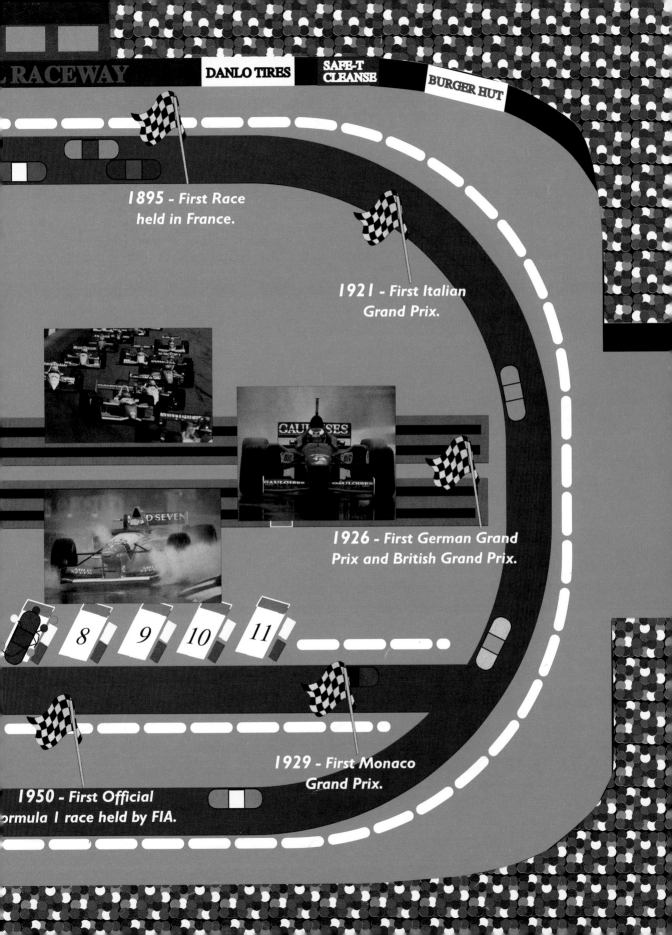

DANLO TIRES

SAFE-T CLEANSE

BURGER HUT

1895 - First Race
held in France.

1921 - First Italian
Grand Prix.

1926 - First German Grand
Prix and British Grand Prix.

8 9 10 11

1929 - First Monaco
Grand Prix.

1950 - First Official
ormula 1 race held by FIA.

–Driver Gear

Each piece of clothing the driver wears must be made of special safety materials. Drivers must wear driving suits which are fireproof. Socks, gloves, shoes, even underwear must also be fireproof. This is to protect the driver in the case of an engine fire while driving or during a crash.

A high-quality helmet is one of the most important pieces of the driver's gear. The helmet could save a driver's life during a crash. Underneath the helmet, a driver wears a balaclava. This looks like a ski mask and is made of special fireproof materials. The helmet has a cable which plugs into a radio so the driver can talk to the crew while on the track. This way, the driver can let the mechanics know if something is wrong with the car while out on the track.

There are also vents in the helmet to keep the driver cool. Most helmets are brightly painted in the driver's favorite colors, or painted to match the car colors. The driver usually places many plastic strips called "tear offs" on the visor of the helmet. If the visor becomes dirty from oil or water from the track, the driver can rip off the disposable plastic strip and see better.

Opposite page: Formula I cars go through many tires during a single race.

–Tire Performance

In Formula 1 racing, tires are very important pieces of equipment. If a tire is worn instead of new, it can be the difference between finishing in 12th place instead of winning the race. Goodyear Eagle racing tires are currently the only type used in Formula 1 racing.

Each driver is given seven sets of dry tires and four sets of wet tires per race weekend. Dry tires are also called slicks. Slicks have smooth surfaces and are designed so the tires grip tight to the track. Wet tires are used if there is rain or the track is moist. These tires look like regular tires with thicker grooves in the center to help move the water out.

The tires are checked constantly. Team mechanics scrub and scrape them to remove pieces of grit, sand, and stone that are caught in the grooves.

Before the tires are used, they are wrapped in electric blankets which are set at a temperature of 110 degrees Fahrenheit so they grip to the track. Warm tires grip the track better and allow the driver to go faster.

–The Days Before the Race

Friday and Saturday morning are spent setting up the car and practicing for the race on Sunday. These days are very critical to the drivers. The driver will be able to tell how well the car will perform on race day based on its performance during practice. The driver can get a feel for the car and tell the team mechanics about any problems the driver is having with the car. The driver wants the car to feel as comfortable as possible.

On practice days, race teams spend time setting up the car. This includes working on the engine, brakes, and handling of the car. The wheels are carefully balanced and the tire pressure is checked. Tire pressures are monitored constantly because they are so critical to lap times.

A wood plank, called the skidblock, is fitted underneath the car. This 10 mm deep wooden plank is used to lower the speeds of the car and is a requirement on all Formula 1 cars. Team mechanics do as much of the work on the cars as possible in an area called the paddock since the pit areas are sometimes very small. The paddock is similar to a garage and is usually away from the track.

Qualifying days take place on the Friday and Saturday afternoons before the race. During this time, the driver and crew chief work closely together to get the best spot in the lineup of cars for the race on Sunday. The crew chief is in charge of the pit crew and helping to prepare the car. The crew chief also works with the engine builder to help gain a competitive edge.

During qualifying, the driver takes 12 laps around the track. Drivers compete for the fastest qualifying speed, which will determine their spot in the lineup.

The driver with the fastest qualifying time has what is called the pole position. This driver will start the race in the front row. Those who do not qualify will end up at the very end of the line. There are a certain amount of spots available for any race. Not every driver will get a spot in the lineup.

After the second qualifying day, the mechanics and engineers spend time fixing and restoring the car to perfect condition so it is ready for the race the next day.

Before a Formula 1 driver can race on the race track, the car must pass an inspection by the race officials who are called scrutineers. Scrutineers perform a 44-point safety check on each car to make sure it is well constructed, with nothing loose or missing on the car. Rules are very strict.

If an item on the car is the wrong size, or made out of the wrong material, the car can be disqualified from the race. The car may be taken away and the driver may have to pay a fine. Rules about the cars are made for the safety of the drivers and to make sure each driver is given a fair chance at competition.

One of the inspections is weighing the car. Each car is pushed onto a ramp with four sets of scales built into it. The new minimum weight for a Formula 1 car is 1,309 pounds (594 kg), including the driver. The scrutineer has each driver's weight on a list, so the driver doesn't need to be there when his car is being weighed.

The inspections used to be held just on Thursday afternoons before the race. However, since some teams have not followed the rules, random tests are held throughout the race weekend.

*Formula 1 cars must pass a strict inspection
before they can get on the track.*

-Race Day

On Sunday, the race teams arrive early and get all the equipment set up in the pits. Last minute repairs are made. All the parts of the car are checked and re-checked to make sure the car is ready to race.

The car is then pushed out to the starting grid, the area on the track where the race will start. The order in which the cars line up is decided during qualifying, the two days before. Marks on the starting grid show where the cars are to be placed.

The pole sitter is placed in the front row in the inside lane. The tires of the cars are usually wrapped in heated blankets to warm the tires so they will grip to the track more quickly. The tires should feel sticky to touch when they are ready.

Dry ice is sometimes placed inside the cars to cool the radiators of the cars as they sit on the starting grid. The radiators may overheat when a car is sitting still for a long time before the race.

After the cars are on the starting grid, the cars must stay in their places until the green flag waves and they cross the start/ finish line. The race itself will take about an hour and a half.

The start of the Molson Indy race in Toronto, Canada in 1997.

−Time For a Pit Stop

It is called a "pit stop" when the driver comes off the track during the race to have repairs made to the car. The driver goes down pit road to the spot where the pit crew is waiting. The pit crew must work together as a team to help get the driver back on the track as soon as possible. Every second a driver spends in the pits can cost the driver several laps on the track.

During a pit stop, tires are changed, fuel is added, and the driver is given a drink of water, all in under 10 seconds! The fastest pit stops can take less than 7 seconds—four and a half for the tires and the rest for refueling. Each team marks a spot on the ground in the pit so the driver will know exactly where to stop the car.

The pit crew practices pit stops many times before the actual race so that they can be as fast as possible. If one member of the team fails to do the job right, or bumps into another team member during a pit stop, it can cost the driver the race. Being on a pit crew can be stressful. Pit stops can win or lose the race.

The pit crew is made up of team members who change tires and add fuel to the car during the race. There are 18 members on

a typical Formula 1 pit crew. There are three people for each tire. Two hold the tire on while the other fastens the wheel with the air wrench.

Two people operate the refueling hose, adding only a certain amount of fuel to the car so it can finish the race. Excess fuel will just weigh the car down. One person jacks up the front of the car and one jacks up the back. The person in front has to be very brave, since a race car will come zooming into the pits, stopping only inches from the front jack operator.

There is an engineer on hand for advice. And finally there is a person who holds out a stick in front of the car and lets the driver know when the pit stop is finished, and it is time to go back onto the track.

Any delays during a pit stop can cost the driver the race.

–Fighting Fire

Sometimes there is the chance that a car could explode into flames on the race track or in the pits. The driver has fireproof clothing on. But what about the pit crew?

The mechanics and other team members wear goggles to protect their eyes. They also wear fireproof overalls and balaclavas, just like the drivers. Those who hold the fuel hose must also wear a fireproof helmet over the balaclava.

If there is a fire, there are specially-trained firefighters at the track to help put out the flames. These people wear shiny, silver, reflective uniforms which are fireproof. They look a lot like aliens from another planet!

Fire is a major hazard in auto racing.

–Timing is Everything

Timing devices are placed in several spots on the race circuit. As cars go past one of the timers, their times are recorded. Average speeds are also flashed up on a screen as the cars pass. This will give the driver an idea of how fast the other cars are going.

Timing sensors are also placed at the entry and exit to the pits, as well as under each race team's pit area. These sensors time how long it takes the pit crew to perform a pit stop. The sensors also tell how long each individual part of a pit stop takes, for example, changing the tires or adding the fuel.

The pit crew tells the driver how well he is doing.

-Victory Lane

When the winner, the second place, and third place finishers cross the finish line, the drivers are said to be in Victory Lane. The three drivers are presented with trophies and prize money. All the hours of preparation were well worth it.

After the race is over, the leading cars are locked in the parc ferme, a secure area in the pits. The cars are checked over to make sure they meet the requirements and that they have not been tampered with during a pit stop. If they pass inspection the cars are released to the teams. Then it's time to take the trophy, pack up the trailer, and head back to the body shop to get the car ready for the next race!

Two drivers congratulate each other after a race.

This driver is headed down victory lane.

–*Glossary*

Air Inlet Duct - A tunnel that looks like a snorkel, which carries air to the engine.

Autoclave - A huge oven used to cook the chassis of the car until it is stiff and strong.

Balaclava - A fireproof piece of clothing that looks like a ski mask. The driver wears this under the helmet for extra protection.

Body - Sheet metal panels of the car which fit over the chassis. The body is hand-crafted most of the time.

Carbon Fiber - The material used to build the chassis of the Formula 1 car.

Chassis - The frame of the car. The chassis is like a skeleton of the car.

Circuit - Another name for race track in Formula 1 racing.

Cockpit - The area of the car where the driver sits.

Crew chief - The crew chief is in charge of organizing the pit crew, overseeing the preparation of the car, and working with the engine builder.

Federation Internationale de l'Automobile - The governing body of the Formula 1 World Championship.

Inconel - An extremely hard steel used for the exhaust pipes.

Inspection - Also called "Scrutineering." All cars must pass requirements for the height, weight, and equipment used in and on the car. Cars are inspected before the race.

Paddock - The area where mechanics work on the race cars. It is similar to a garage and is usually away from the track.

Pit crew - Members of the race team who help change tires and refuel during the race.

Pit stop - When the driver needs new tires or more fuel, the driver comes off the track during the race and makes a pit stop.

Pole position - The best spot to start the race. The pole position is won by the driver who had the fastest time during qualifying.

Qualifying - During qualifying, drivers compete for the fastest qualifying speed, which will determine their spot in the lineup of the race.

Safety Harness - The special seat belt which keeps the driver from moving around while racing.

Skidblock - Wood plank which is placed underneath the car to help lower the speed and downforce of the car.

Starting Grid - The area on the track where the cars line up to begin the race.

Tear-offs - Disposable plastic strips the driver places on the visor of the helmet. If the visor gets dirty, the driver just tears off the strip.

Tire pressure - The amount of air that is put in the tire. In stock car racing, all four tires could have different amounts of air.

Transporter - The large, fancy truck used to transport Formula 1 cars to races.

Truckies - Drivers and mechanics of the transporter trucks that transport the race cars from race to race.

–Internet Sites

Formula 1 Links Heaven
http://ireland.iol.ie/~roym/
This site includes official sites, latest news, drivers, teams, computer games, circuits, mailing lists. This site has sound and video, very colorful and interactive.

Drag Racing on the net
http://www.lm.com/~hemi/
This is a cool and interactive sight with sound and fun photos.

Indyphoto.com
http://www.indyphoto.com/index.htm
This award winning site has excellent photographs of Indy Cars and it is updated on a regular basis.

MotorSports Image Online
http://www.msimage.com/index2.htm
This site gives you standings, results, schedules, teams, news, and a photo gallery.

Extreme Off-Road Racing
http://www.calpoly.edu/~jcallan/
This site has pre-runners, chat rooms, videos, racing pictures, wrecks, links, and much more extreme off-road racing stuff.

These sites are subject to change. Go to your favorite search engine and type in car racing for more sites.

Pass It On

Racing Enthusiasts: educate readers around the country by passing on information you've learned about car racing. Share your little-known facts and interesting stories. Tell others what your favorite kind of car is or who your favorite racer is. We want to hear from you!

To get posted on the ABDO & Daughters website E-mail us at "Sports@abdopub.com"

Visit the ABDO & Daughter website at www.abdopub.com

–Index